USA TODAY. **TEEN WISE GUIDES**

A GANNETT COMPANY

LIFESTYLE CHOICES

SAFETY

SMARTS

How to Manage Threats, Protect Yourself, Get Help, and More

MATT DOEDEN

TWENTY-FIRST CENTURY BOOKS / MINNEAPOLIS

USA TODAY Snapshots®, graphics, and excerpts from USA TODAY articles quoted on back cover and on pp. 8, 10–11, 24, 30–31, 40–41, 43, 45, 51, 52–53 © copyright 2013 by USA TODAY.

Twenty-First Century Books
A division of Lerner Publishing Group, Inc.
241 First Avenue North
Minneapolis, MN 55401 U.S.A.

Website address: www.lernerbooks.com

Library of Congress Cataloging-in-Publication Data

Doeden, Matt.
  Safety Smarts : how to manage threats, protect yourself, get help, and more / by Matt Doeden.
      p. cm. — (USA TODAY teen wise guides : lifestyle choices)
  Includes bibliographical references and index.
  ISBN 978-0-7613-7022-2 (lib. bdg. : alk. paper)
  1. Safety education. 2. Teenagers—Crimes against—Prevention. I. Title.
  HQ770.7.D64 2013
  613.6083'5—dc23   2011044268

The images in this book are used with the permission of: © weareadventures/Vetta/Getty Images, p. 4; © OMG/Photodisc/Getty Images, p. 5; © Gary S. Chapman/Photographer's Choice/Getty Images, p. 6 (left); © Keith Muccilli/ East Brunswick Home News Tribune/USA TODAY, pp. (6-7); © George Doyle/Stockbyte/Getty Images, p. 8 (bottom); © DorianGray/Vetta/Getty Images, p. 9; © Shannon Fagan/The Image Bank/Getty Images, p. 11; © Karen Moskowitz/Stone/Getty Images, p. 12; © Nikolay Titov/Vetta/Getty Images, p. 13; © Rubberball/Mike Kemp/Getty Images, pp. 14, 29; © Jose Luis Pelaez Inc/Blend Images/Getty Images, p. 15; © Kablonk! RM/Golden Pixels LCC/Alamy, p. 16; © DreamsPictures/Blend Images/Getty Images, p. 18 (left); © John Giustina/Iconica/Getty Images, pp. (18-19); © Paul Edmondson/Photodisc/Getty Images, p. 20; © PhotoAlto Agency RF Collections/Getty Images, p. 21; © Darrin Klimek/Digital Vision/Getty Images, p. 22; © Chomorange/Raider Peter/Alamy, p. 23; © Will & Deni McIntyre/CORBIS, p. 26; AP Photo/The Star Tribune/Brue Bisping, p. 27; © Fuse/Getty Images, p. 28; © Vstock LLC/ Getty Images, p. 31; © Brendan O'Sulivan/Photolibrary/Getty Images, p. 33; © Nicole Hill/Getty Images, p. 34; © ImageSource/ Getty Images, p. 36 (left); © Jessica Miller/Workbook Stock/Getty Images, pp. 36-37; © Sami Sarkis/Photographer's Choice/ Getty Images, p. 38; © LWA/Jay Newman/Blend Images/Getty Images, p. 39; © Anna Peisl/CORBIS, p. 41; © Felix Mizionikov/ Dreamstime.com, p. 44; Jeffery Phelps/MCT/Newscom, p. 46; Zuma Press/Newscom, p. 48 (left); © Jon Riley/Photolibrary/ Getty Images, pp. 48-49; © Laurence Mouton/PhotoAlto Agency RF Collections/Getty Images, p. 50; © Todd Strand/Independent Picture Service, p. 53; © Hill Street Studios/Matthew Palmer/Blend Images/Getty Images, p. 54; © Matt Rainey/Star Ledger/ CORBIS, p. 55; AP Photo/Katsumi Kasahara, p. 57; © Yellow Dog Productions/The Image Bank/Getty Images, p. 58. Front cover: © David Hannah/Photolibrary/Getty Images.

Main body text set in Conduit ITC Std 11/15
Typeface provided by International Typeface Corp

Manufactured in the United States of America
1 – PP – 7/15/12

CONTENTS

Maria looked over her shoulder. The man in the long coat was still half a block behind her. He'd been following her since she left school. Normally she walked home with friends. But today she'd had to stay late to work on a science project. It was getting dark, and her heart was racing.

Not all text messages are friendly. Be aware that some people who contact you might have bad intentions.

It had been a scary week. First, a stranger had tried to friend her on Facebook. Next, she started getting creepy texts from someone she didn't know. And her phone had rung several times, but nobody was on the other end when she answered. Now this.

Maria turned a corner, hoping the stranger wouldn't follow. But sure enough, he turned the corner too. And he was getting closer. She was starting to panic.

What should Maria do? Should she run? Confront the man following her? Scream at the top of her lungs for help? Reach for her cell phone?

You have to make choices about your safety every day. They may not be as dramatic as the ones Maria has to make, but they're still important. Do you reply to that suspicious text or just ignore it? Do you stand up to a bully or walk away from the situation? Do you walk home alone at night or call a parent for a ride? How do you steer clear of danger while still living your life? It's a tough balance to strike. Keep reading for some ideas on how to do it.

1 REDUCING *Your Risk*

Most things in life, such as driving a car and playing sports, come with a risk. You can lessen the risk by using safety smarts.

Sometimes it seems as if danger is everywhere—on the street, in school, on the Internet, and even in your own home. But don't freak out. With some smarts and a healthy dose of awareness, you can make a lot of those threats disappear. Managing threats is all about the choices you make. Many things in life come with risk. And we're not just talking about skydiving or mountain climbing here. Riding a bike comes with the risk of falling. When you get behind the wheel of a car, you're risking an accident. Playing sports comes with the risk of being injured. Even going to school might come with the risk of being bullied.

Accepting some risk is a part of life. The trick is knowing how to understand, manage, and live with risks. After all, we can't lock ourselves away and shut out the world. The key is living the life you want to lead while *minimizing the dangers that life brings.*

USA TODAY Snapshots®

Why teens don't drink and drive

40%
It's dangerous

33%
It's stupid/ wrong

32%
For own safety

26%
Don't drink

10%
It's against the law

Source: SADD and Liberty Mutual Group

By Cindy Hall and Quin Tian, USA TODAY, 2001

Most teens know that drinking and driving is a bad move. Life is risky enough without adding drunken driving to the mix.

If you have to walk alone in the dark, consider carrying a can of pepper spray.

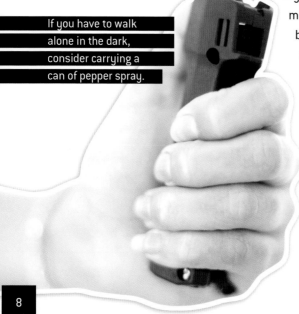

If you want to go for a drive, make sure to wear your seat belt, pay attention to what you're doing, and follow traffic rules. Just like that, your risk goes way down. The same is true with other risky situations. Don't go walking down a strange, dark alley at night. If you must go out alone at night, carry a can of pepper spray or a rape whistle. If you see a guy spoiling for a fight, don't provoke him. Walk away. In most situations, a little common sense goes a long way.

TRUST YOUR GUT:
AWARENESS AND INSTINCT

Ever spend time watching toddlers? Often they stumble through life without really understanding what's going on around them. They might put toys into their mouths, walk straight into furniture, grab sharp objects, or rush up to greet complete strangers. Adults have to watch toddlers constantly, because the little ones aren't very aware of their surroundings. They don't know how to recognize and avoid danger.

Toddlers have to be watched by an adult because they haven't learned how to avoid danger. But as a teenager, you have developed an instinct for what might be dangerous.

SUMMERTIME CAN BE THE BREAKING POINT FOR TEEN SAFETY

By Kim Painter

What do you get when you combine fine weather, freedom and the carefree exuberance of youth? Many teens and young adults get something that their parents remember fondly: a real summer break, full of fun and friends. But the truth is, some also get into trouble. "The hundred deadliest days for teen drivers and teen passengers" are between Memorial Day and Labor Day, says Justin McNaull, director of state relations for AAA [American Automobile Association] auto clubs.

Emergency-room doctors know these months as "trauma season," and they expect a long, hot parade of injured drivers, boaters, swimmers, bikers and partiers, many of whom will be in their teens and 20s and will be under the influence of alcohol or drugs, says Sandra Schneider, an emergency-room doctor in Rochester, N.Y., and president of the American College of Emergency Physicians.

In summer, "for many teens, every day is a Saturday," free of responsibility and full of unsupervised hours to spend with friends, often in cars, McNaull says. "Car crashes are the leading cause of death, by a mile," for teens year-round, he says, but summer is especially deadly.

From 2005 to 2009, more than 7,300 passengers and drivers ages 13 to 19 were killed in crashes between Memorial Day and Labor Day, and an average of 422 died in each summer month compared with an average of 363 in non-summer months, a new analysis by AAA shows. One explanation: Teenagers spend more hours driving in summer (44% more, according to a study from Liberty Mutual and Students Against Destructive Decisions). And they often "ride with passengers on what we call 'purposeless trips,'" McNaull says.

He recommends that parents and teenagers revisit car-related rules in the summer. Parents should limit non-essential driving and make sure their teens, even those too young to drive, know that it's a bad idea to ride with inexperienced teenage drivers. More suggestions can be found at TeenDriving.AAA.com.

Road trips are fun, especially in summer, but they can also be dangerous for teen drivers.

But teens and young adults don't need a car to get hurt, especially if they've been drinking, Schneider says: "We often think of impaired drivers, but we also see impaired boaters and water skiers," young women sexually assaulted while drunk, and young people poisoned in bouts of binge drinking.

Those are the things many parents fear as high school grads head off for [summer] trips with friends. When her daughter went to Myrtle Beach, S.C., several years ago, [Nancy] Hans says, they agreed she would carry her cellphone at all times and pick up when her mother called at least once a day. Other parents kept similarly close tabs on other kids in the group, she says, "and I was relieved that everybody came back safely."

—*June 7, 2011*

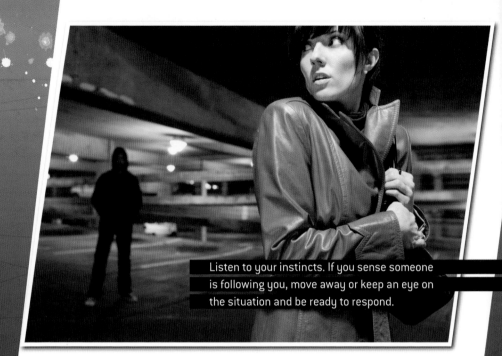

Listen to your instincts. If you sense someone is following you, move away or keep an eye on the situation and be ready to respond.

Lucky for you, you're not a toddler. You're aware of your surroundings. But really knowing what's going on around you takes some work and attention. You'll need to notice how people are acting toward one another and toward you, especially if someone seems to be paying you extra or unwanted attention—such as the man following Maria as she walked home from school. If a situation doesn't seem quite right, move away—or at least keep an eye on it. That way, if something bad happens, you'll be ready to respond.

Part of being aware is listening to your own instincts. What exactly is an instinct? It's a gut feeling. It's something you sense, even if your mind can't come up with a rational reason for it. Did you ever just get a funny feeling about someone or a feeling that a situation wasn't quite right? That's an instinct. Some part of your mind may have noticed a sign of danger, even if you weren't consciously aware of it. *If in doubt, follow your instincts.*

Your gut is trying to tell you something. Listen to it—even if it means you have to be rude. Being safe is more important than being polite.

IMAGE IS EVERYTHING

A lot of the dangers we face come from other people. Most bullies, muggers, sexual predators, and other unsavory folks choose their targets carefully. Believe it or not, the way you look and act can have a big impact on whether they'll choose you. **Your appearance and actions send out an image** to the rest of the world.

Imagine two boys walking through the halls at school. One kid shuffles along with little steps. His shoulders are slumped, and his head is down. He won't make eye contact and seems

Even if you feel down and lack confidence, don't let a bully know it.

Don't project the image of a victim. Act confident and be friendly with your classmates.

to want to avoid everyone. Now imagine a second kid. He walks purposefully, with his head up and shoulders back. He takes long, confident strides. He's looking at the people around him, smiling, waving, and saying hello.

Which kid do you think looks like a better target for a bully? You got it—the first one. When bullies look for victims, they often pick people who look shy or vulnerable. The same is true on the street with muggers, sexual predators, and other folks up to no good.

The idea here is simple. If you project the image of a victim, you're more likely to become one. *Try to look confident*—even if you're not feeling very confident. Keep your head up and your back straight. Look people in the eye. Nothing projects confidence better. Don't hold your arms tight against your body. That makes you look as if you're cowering. Keep your shoulders square to your body. This posture not only projects confidence but also leaves you ready to react quickly.

Of course, if someone is intent on trying to harm you, all the good posture in the world probably won't change his or her mind. But in many cases, simply projecting the right image will be enough to ward off trouble.

SPEAK UP

Being aware and projecting an image aren't always enough. If you find yourself threatened, it's time to use your voice—loudly if need be. Imagine you're out alone at night. You're walking down the street when you hear footsteps behind you. You turn and see someone approaching you. Before you realize what's happening, a stranger has grabbed you by the wrist. What now?

Simple changes, such as standing up straight, can help project a strong image and can help ward off bullying.

15

You have several options. You could fight, or you could flee. But a good place to start is with the magic word "Help!" Few attackers want an audience for their crimes. Calling attention to yourself might be enough to get the attacker to run off.

Other situations aren't so simple. Imagine that an adult or a classmate is touching you inappropriately or making unwanted sexual remarks. The first thing to do is to tell the person that you're uncomfortable, since he or she might not even realize how you feel. Be direct. "You're making me uncomfortable" is a good starting place. If that doesn't work, you can try a firm and loud "Stop!" And if that doesn't do the trick, it's probably time to look for help. Talk to a trusted adult about the situation.

If someone is making unwanted sexual remarks or moves, tell the person you feel uncomfortable.

DEFINING
THE DANGER

Threats can take a lot of forms. Check out these definitions of various types of dangers to get a handle on what's what.

abduction: the taking and kidnapping of a person against his or her will

abuse: physical or verbal mistreatment of another person, usually with the abuser being in a position of authority (such as a teacher abusing a student or a boss abusing an employee)

assault: a physical attack on another person

domestic abuse: abuse carried out between members of a family or a household

domestic assault: a violent physical attack against a member of one's family or household

hate crime: an attack on a person based on bias against his or her race, ethnicity, sexual orientation, religion, or other social characteristic

rape: a violent attack in which the attacker forces sexual intercourse on the victim

sexual abuse: inappropriate and unwelcome sexual contact, usually with the abuser being in a position of authority

sexual assault: a violent attack in which the attacker forces a sexual act upon the victim

stalking: when one person follows and watches the activities of another. A stalker may make unwelcome phone calls; show up at a victim's home, work, or school; or even contact a victim's friends or family.

2 SAFETY EVERYWHERE *You Go*

Most social situations are pretty safe for teens—especially when you're with a group of friends. But don't let your guard down completely.

Your life is probably pretty busy. You spend a lot of time at home and at school. You might spend time on the Internet, hanging out at the mall, or chilling out at the local pool. Every setting comes with its own dangers. If you stay aware of where you are, what's going on around you, and who else is there, you've got a good start. But for some more safety tips, keep reading.

SAFETY AT HOME

Home is supposed to be a safe place, right? You've got the comforts of family, your own bed, and maybe your own room. And it's true—your home is probably a pretty safe place. You've got locks on the door to keep out strangers, smoke alarms to let you know if there's a fire, and family members to watch over you. But that doesn't mean you should let your guard down entirely. Even at home, you've got to stay safe. Threats can sometimes come from people you know and love, including physical or sexual abuse from family members or friends. Or

Use your telephone wisely. Never let a caller know you're home alone. And if you're feeling threatened, use the phone to call for help.

they can come from strangers, especially if you're home alone.

What do you do if the doorbell rings and you look out the front window and see a stranger? Do you just open up and say hello? Not for a stranger. Instead, call a parent or another adult to the door. If you're home alone, you can talk with the stranger through the closed door. Ask who it is and what he or she wants. No matter what the stranger says, tell him or her you're not interested. Someone up to no good might make up a story to lure you outside. Maybe he or she will ask for directions or for help with a stalled car. Don't get sucked in. Most adults would never ask kids they don't know for help.

What you shouldn't do is tell a stranger that your parents are away. Never invite a stranger inside or step outside, where you might be putting yourself in harm's way. If someone continues to try to get inside after you've asked him or her to leave, it's probably time to call for help. Contact a neighbor or even the police, depending on the level of threat you feel.

What about a similar situation on the telephone? A stranger is calling, asking for your parents, who are out. Do you tell the caller that you're home alone? That's not a great idea. A better idea is to say that

If someone breaks into your house while you're home alone, try to exit safely through a back door or a window.

your parents are busy and to ask for a number where they can call back. If your parents have a cell phone, you can call and give them the message right away. Otherwise, write it down for when they return.

Suppose you're home when someone breaks in. Now what? Experts say the first thing to do is to *get to a safe place*. If you can safely sneak out a back door or a window, go for it. Otherwise, grab a cell phone if you have one and then hide in a bathroom, a closet, the basement, or some other out-of-the-way place. Use your phone to call 911 for help. If you don't have a phone, stay put and remain quiet until the intruder is gone.

If you find yourself face-to-face with the intruder, try not to panic. Don't grab for a baseball bat or other weapon. The intruder is more likely to hurt you if he or she sees you as a threat. Try to speak calmly. Don't scream. The more panicked you are, the more the intruder is likely to panic—bad news for you. If the intruder is simply trying to rob you, don't put up a fight. Possessions are replaceable. Your life isn't.

SAFETY AT SCHOOL

School is another place where you really should feel safe. After all, you're surrounded by friends, teachers, and other responsible adults. But the truth is that for many kids, school doesn't always feel safe. Bullying is a big problem in schools. Verbal or physical abuse at the hands of a bully can be devastating. Bullied kids can feel embarrassed, ashamed, angry, depressed, or even suicidal. That's no laughing matter.

Why do kids bully? Some bullies are just looking for attention. Picking on other kids may seem like a way to become popular. Others want to feel important or powerful. They may feel victimized and vulnerable in other parts of their lives—at home, in the classroom, or elsewhere—so they try to gain a sense of power by picking on someone else.

Don't let bullies get under your skin. A bully might try to get a rise out of you. Don't give him or her the satisfaction.

What should you do if you're the target of a bully? That depends on your personality and the situation. If it's just a one-time thing, it may be best to simply walk away or to respond with indifference. The bully might be trying to get you to react. If you give the bully that emotional reaction, you might be setting yourself up for more abuse. Take a breath and shrug your shoulders. If you look as if you're not interested, the bully might move on.

The same basic idea holds true for more persistent bullying. Remember, bullies are trying to get an emotional response out of you. Don't give it to them! Some experts recommend keeping a private journal where you can write about how you feel and how the bullying is affecting you. When you write, you can be as emotional as you want. But when face-to-face with a bully, try to keep a level head. Don't show that emotional reaction the bully is looking for.

If the bullying continues, take some simple steps to protect yourself. Stay with groups of friends. Most bullies will be reluctant to harass or attack

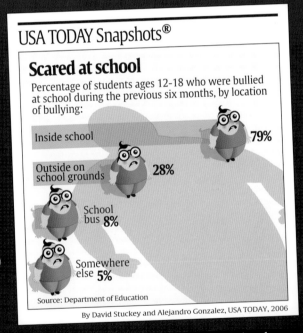

USA TODAY Snapshots®

Scared at school

Percentage of students ages 12-18 who were bullied at school during the previous six months, by location of bullying:

Inside school — 79%

Outside on school grounds — 28%

School bus — 8%

Somewhere else — 5%

Source: Department of Education

By David Stuckey and Alejandro Gonzalez, USA TODAY, 2006

School should be a safe place, yet the majority of kids who are bullied say that the bullying happens at school.

HATE CRIMES

If you watch the news, you've probably heard the term *hate crime*. A hate crime is an attack on a person based on a bias against his or her race, ethnicity, sexual orientation, religion, or other social characteristic. Hate crimes are motivated by prejudice.

Sometimes kids are the victims of hate crimes. At school, bullies might threaten or attack someone of a racial or religious minority. Sometimes attackers target teenagers who are gay—or who are thought to be gay. Hate crimes are serious offenses. Victims have been seriously injured and even murdered.

If you see a hate crime happening or if you are the victim of a hate crime, seek help immediately. Nobody should have to suffer simply for being who they are.

somebody in a large group. In class, don't sit in the back. Sit up front near the teacher, so he or she can easily see any bullying taking place. Also sit near the front of the school bus, close to the bus driver. Remind yourself that you're a good person who doesn't deserve to be picked on. Remember that the bully is probably picking on you because something's lacking in his or her own life.

If your bully is really getting to you—either with insults or with physical attacks—seek help. Talk to your parents, a teacher, the school psychologist or principal, or another trusted adult. Depending on the situation, the adult may talk directly to the bully or to the bully's parents, who may choose to punish him or her. Teachers and other school staff can also keep a close eye on the situation on school grounds and punish the bully if necessary.

If a bully is really bothering you, talk to an adult you trust.

But if you've reported the situation to adults and the bullying still doesn't stop, there's always a last resort. Talk to your parents about changing schools. It's a drastic move, but if there's no other way to end the bullying, you may find it's worth the effort. **You deserve to feel safe at school.**

SAFETY IN PUBLIC PLACES

You probably don't want to lock yourself away at home all day. That means going out among people—including strangers—and dealing with a whole new set of risks. When you're out in public— whether it's at a school football game, at the mall, or just hanging out on your own street—stay aware.

First, be aware of where you are. Public places with a lot of people are usually safest. If a criminal plans to rob or attack someone, the best place to do it will have few or no witnesses. So for you, a busy mall is probably safer than an abandoned street or an empty park. The time of day is also important. A public street that's perfectly safe in the daytime might not be so safe late at night, when most people have gone home.

Criminals don't like an audience. If you're surrounded by friends and schoolmates, you're more likely to be safe.

Next, remember that there's safety in numbers. Go out with friends or family whenever possible, especially if you're going out at night. Large groups aren't attractive targets for attackers. Even being with just one other person is a whole lot safer than being alone.

If you do feel threatened in public, remember to use your voice. Shout if you have to. Call attention to yourself. Remember: an attacker doesn't want witnesses. The more you can draw attention to yourself, the safer you'll be.

DOG ATTACK!

We've spent a lot of time talking about threats from other people. But what if you're walking down the sidewalk, minding your own business, and suddenly find yourself staring a strange, growling dog in the face? You can't reason with the animal, and it probably won't be satisfied with your wallet. So what do you do? Most dogs won't bite you. They may growl and lunge but never actually bite. But most isn't *all.* So you've got to know what to do.

Remember that thousands of years ago, before people started living with dogs, cats, and farm animals, dogs were wild animals. They lived in packs. Even though dogs are no longer wild, they still have a pack mentality. For many dogs, people are just part of the pack. So you need to show an aggressive dog that you're above it on the pack's chain of command. That means standing tall and holding your ground. If you cower or run, the dog may see that as weakness and an invitation to bite. Use your voice and show the dog who's boss. Most dogs know the command "NO!" If your voice is firm and authoritative, most dogs will take notice. If you know the dog's name, use it. That will certainly get its attention. Then walk—don't run—calmly away.

If you do get bitten, seek medical help immediately. Dogs can carry dangerous diseases such as rabies. You'll want to report to the police where the bite happened and what kind of dog bit you. If you know who the dog's owners are, report that as well. If the dog's shots aren't up to date, you may need to get extra medical care to prevent disease.

SAFETY ON THE ROAD

Maybe you or your friends are driving already. If not, the time isn't far away. Driving comes with a whole new set of dangers and responsibilities. A moving vehicle is basically a weapon. You've got to treat it with the same care and attention you'd give a loaded gun.

You've heard all about the dangers of driving under the influence of alcohol or drugs. There's only one way to tackle this safety problem: don't do it. Don't do it yourself, don't let your friends do it, and by all means, don't climb into a car if the driver's been drinking or using drugs. Instead, call a parent or another trusted adult for a ride.

What you may not have heard as much about is distracted driving. What is distracted driving? It's driving a vehicle while not giving the road your full attention. Things like talking on your phone, texting, putting on makeup, or even talking with friends can take your attention from the road. And all it takes is a second or two of inattention to lead to tragedy.

Imagine you're driving down the road and trying to send a text. You may look down for only a moment, but in that moment, a little girl runs into the road in front of you. You never see the child because you were focused on the phone. At the last moment, you see her in front of you and slam on the brakes. You might stop in time—but you might not.

If someone gets hurt—or killed—because of your distracted driving, you'll regret it for the rest of your life. Do yourself and everyone else a favor. When you're driving, *give the road your full attention*. There will be plenty of time for talking, texting, and other activities later.

USA TODAY
News
SECTION A
NEWS.USATODAY.COM

"AWARENESS GAP"
ON ROAD TEXTING

By Larry Copeland

Many teens view texting while driving as less risky than drunken driving despite a sustained campaign against texting behind the wheel and research indicating it's as dangerous as drinking and driving, a new survey for State Farm insurance company finds. "We're doing everything possible to get the message out to teens that driving while talking or texting on a cellphone is not worth the risk," says Transportation Secretary Ray LaHood. "Teen drivers are some of the most vulnerable drivers on the road due to inexperience, and adding cellphones to the mix only compounds the dangers," LaHood says.

The survey comes after more than two years of a national campaign against distracted driving, especially texting. LaHood has made it a signature issue of his tenure [time in office], talk show host Oprah Winfrey regularly urges her millions of viewers not to do it, and 30 states have banned it, including 10 this year.

Yet there remains "a real awareness gap around the dangers of distracted driving, and that's what we heard in this survey," says Laurette Stiles, State Farm's vice president of strategic resources. "The risks and the dangers are not well understood by teens. I believe that one of the reasons is that they're not well understood by parents, either." A University of Utah study found that cellphone use caused distractions for motorists as serious as driving with a blood-alcohol content of 0.08%, the legal definition of driving while intoxicated.

The State Farm survey highlights a reality of life among many teens: Staying connected is vitally important to them, and maintaining that connection—even when they're driving—overrides safety warnings from driver's education instructors, celebrities and even parents. Just ask Connor, 18, who rear-ended another car in October while sending a text message to a friend.

"It (staying connected) is very important, probably more important than it should be," says Connor. "My parents were very serious about me not texting

Texting while driving is very dangerous and illegal in some states. Don't risk it—put the phone down and concentrate on the road.

and driving. But when you text somebody, if they don't respond in five minutes, you start to wonder what happened, what's wrong."

Although teens might not yet fully grasp the risks of road texting, the focus on distracted driving is making many motorists more wary. The AAA [American Automobile Association] Foundation for Traffic Safety says 52% of drivers in its new survey feel less safe than they did five years ago—a 17-percentage-point increase since the same time last year; 40% of these drivers cited cellphones/texting/distracted drivers as the biggest reason they feel unsafe.

— *September 20, 2010*

SAFETY ON THE INTERNET

You probably know that the Internet is full of hazards. It's swimming with harmful software called viruses and malware. These annoying little computer programs can wreak havoc on your machine, causing lots of damage to your files or even stealing your personal information. But did you know that your own safety can be at risk on the Internet too? Cyberbullies can harass you, spread nasty rumors about you, or post embarrassing photos of you on social media sites. Cyberstalkers are even worse. They may follow your every online move to gather information about you, such as where you live and hang out. Then they might stalk you in person. The worst of the worst are sexual predators who search online for victims. With all of that going on, you've got to keep up your guard.

Just as in real life, being prepared and aware can make all the difference in online safety. Know who you're chatting with, which can be tough since many people don't use their real names online. If you aren't sure who's on the other end of a chat window, watch for odd behavior, uncomfortable personal questions, or anything else that seems suspicious. If in doubt, log off and talk to an adult.

Imagine a teenager named Lily, chatting away in a room devoted to an alternative band. She meets someone, who claims to be a girl her age and living just one town over. They agree to meet after school. Lily suggests a local burger place, but her new friend insists that Lily come to her house instead. Sound like trouble? You bet it is! There's no way for Lily to know who she's really going to see. It might not even be another teenage girl at all. It might be a sexual predator.

The lesson here is that if someone you meet online wants to meet in person, use your head. If you do agree to meet, don't go to a private home. Meet in public—in the middle of a shopping mall or at a restaurant. And always take a trusted adult with you to the meeting. The adult doesn't have to be standing there when you meet your online friend, but he or she should be nearby just in case.

Also remember to *guard your personal information online.* Keep your name, phone number, address, hometown, and even e-mail address private. Be aware that a cyberstalker might be able to find you at home with even a small piece of information, such as an e-mail address. On sites such as Facebook, be aware that people on your friends list might have access to some of this personal data. So if someone you don't know tries to friend you, deny the request.

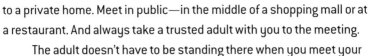

Your Facebook friends could access your personal data, so make sure you accept friend requests only from people you trust.

Many social networking sites allow you to report unwelcome friend requests with the click of a button. Use it! This tool helps protect everyone in the network.

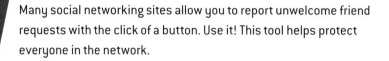

SAFETY AND S-E-X

Chuckle and smirk all you like—safety and sex is a big deal. We're not talking about a little smooching with a boyfriend or girlfriend here—we're talking about your body and how to protect it. Remember that it's *your* body, nobody else's. You're the only one who should be making decisions about how

When it comes to sex, know your limits and stand up for yourself.

it's treated. *Nobody has the right to touch you in ways that make you uncomfortable in any way*—not classmates, friends, teachers, or family members. Not anyone.

What do you do if someone is making you uncomfortable? Talk with the person clearly and firmly. Make sure the person understands exactly why his or her words or actions are making you uncomfortable. If that doesn't solve the problem, talk with a parent or another trusted adult about the situation.

What if someone is being sexually aggressive and there's no one nearby to help? What if your words aren't stopping the advances? It's time to defend yourself. Start by screaming to get some attention. If you have to bite, kick, claw, punch, or pull hair to get free, do it. Then get away as fast as you can and seek help.

Remember, if you're a victim of sexual abuse of any kind, it's not your fault. There's nothing to be embarrassed about. **Never be afraid to ask for help.**

Even when sex is consensual, or agreed upon by both partners, you still need to protect yourself. Use a condom to protect against sexually transmitted diseases and sexually transmitted infections (STDs and STIs). Condoms and other birth control methods usually will protect against unwanted pregnancies. Going into a drugstore to buy condoms may seem embarrassing, but going to a doctor to get treated for an STD or an STI is a whole lot more embarrassing. And becoming a teen parent could drastically change your plans for college, a career, and pretty much everything else about the rest of your life.

3 FIGHT OR *Flight*

If you do get attacked, don't panic. If you use your head, you can get away unharmed.

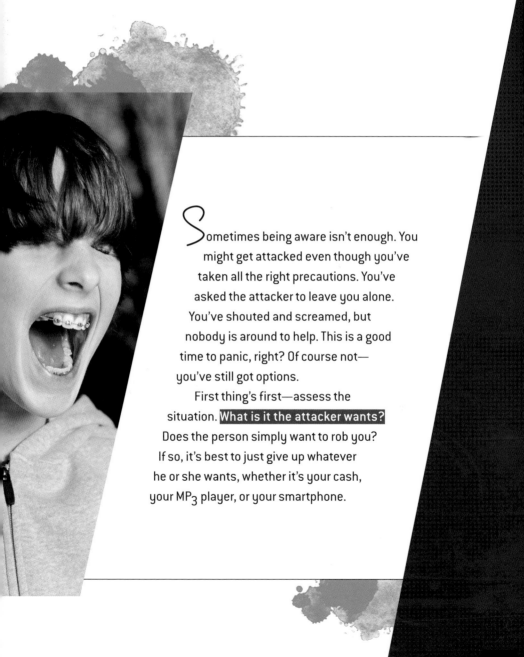

Sometimes being aware isn't enough. You might get attacked even though you've taken all the right precautions. You've asked the attacker to leave you alone. You've shouted and screamed, but nobody is around to help. This is a good time to panic, right? Of course not—you've still got options.

First thing's first—assess the situation. What is it the attacker wants? Does the person simply want to rob you? If so, it's best to just give up whatever he or she wants, whether it's your cash, your MP$_3$ player, or your smartphone.

Money and objects can be replaced. The same can't be said for your life. But if your attacker seems intent on hurting you or taking you somewhere against your will, you'll have some decisions to make.

If an attacker does not have a hold on you, run away as fast as you can.

THE BEST OPTION: ESCAPE

Your first option when attacked should always be to get away from the dangerous situation as quickly as you can. In other words, RUN! If your attacker doesn't have a hold of you, turn tail and get out of there as fast as your feet will carry you. **Shout for help as you run.** Look for anyone who could be of help—neighbors, police officers, security guards, or other authority figures. If all you see are strangers, **pick someone who looks trustworthy.** Some experts recommend finding a mother with children. She's very likely to be trustworthy.

What if an attacker has a hold of you? Escape may still be an option. If your attacker has grabbed you by the wrist, there's a simple way to **break the grip.** Rotate your arm in a wide circle, so that the movement presses against your attacker's thumb. If you apply enough pressure, the thumb should bend back, releasing you from the grip. If you manage to make this trick work, don't stand around admiring yourself. Hightail it out of there immediately.

When you are running away from an attacker, look for someone trustworthy to help you, such as a mother with children.

KIDS RUN, SHOUT, FIGHT—ALL FOIL ABDUCTIONS

By Wendy Koch

Stephanie recalls walking to school on a sunny morning in Albany, N.Y., last year when, a block from school, a man grabbed her from behind. He put a towel over her face. She screamed for help. "Shut up! Shut up!" he ordered. "I have a knife. I'll stab you."

"He was trying to force me to walk with him, but I kept fighting him," says Stephanie, then 14. Two men working nearby heard her yell and ran to help.

The attacker dropped the towel and ran off. DNA [genetic material] on the towel linked Darius Ashley to her assault and to the abduction and rape of two other young women. He's now serving a 25-year prison sentence.

Stephanie's case fits the pattern of most attempted abductions, according to a study released by the National Center for Missing & Exploited Children. The typical victim is a teenage girl on her way to or from school.

The study, released as a new school year gets under way, examined 403 attempted kidnappings by strangers or slight acquaintances that were reported by police or news media in 45 states from February 2005 to July 2006. It was conducted to learn how such attempts are foiled [defeated]. The study did not look at successful abductions.

Six in 10 victims fought back and escaped, according to the ongoing study's initial findings. Three in 10 ran away before any physical contact, and about 10% were saved when an adult nearby intervened.

"It is more important than ever for parents to empower their kids," says Ernie Allen, the center's president. He says he doesn't want to scare children, but they need to learn to recognize danger and, if attacked, draw attention by screaming, kicking and running away.

"We look for patterns," Allen says. "These guys [attackers] don't do it just once. An attempt is likely to be followed by another and another until they're successful." That's why he wants parents to report incidents to police.

Robert Kemmet, a detective with the Oklahoma City Police Department, has studied 170 local kidnapping attempts and says identifying patterns

When faced with a fight-or-flight decision, flight is usually the best option.

has led to several arrests. "We can create an environment that makes it very difficult for a predator to operate," says Kemmet, who orders extra surveillance [monitoring] when he knows of an area where someone has repeatedly approached children. He cites common lures: "Hey, little girl, do you want a piece of candy?" Or "Can you help me look for my puppy?" Some predators, he says, are "bus trawlers" who drive behind a school bus, watching for a child to get off alone. "That's what the predator is counting on: the lone child," Kemmet says.

Stephanie has recovered from her near-abduction. She is a high school sophomore who plays soccer and basketball. She testified at her attacker's trial and says she's willing to talk about what happened: "It's a way for me to use it to help other kids."

Now Stephanie walks to school with friends when she doesn't get a ride. She never walks alone.

—*September 6, 2006*

ADRENALINE RUSH

Has a friend ever popped out from behind a corner and shouted "BOO!" at you? You might have jumped back, gasped, or even screamed in surprise. Your friend probably had a good chuckle at your expense, but your body was kicking off a critical survival response called fight or flight. When you're confronted with danger (or even a sudden surprise), chemicals called adrenaline and cortisol surge into your bloodstream, providing a short, sudden burst of energy. Your muscles tense, and your heart rate soars. This is the body's way of preparing to quickly respond to the threat. For a few moments, you're amped up for action— fight or flight. This might not seem like a particularly useful response to a friend who is just trying to scare you, but it has helped human beings survive in a dangerous world for millions of years.

THE LAST RESORT: FIGHT

What if escape isn't an option? It might be time to fight. But you've got to decide whether fighting is likely to help you or hurt you. For example, if your attacker has a gun, fighting might persuade him or her to pull the trigger. In any situation, you'll have to rely on your instincts to tell you what to do. *Remember, if in doubt, go with your gut.*

How exactly are you supposed to go about fighting? Do you put up your dukes and challenge your attacker to a good old-fashioned fistfight? Of course not. At this point, you're not interested in fighting fair. Your only goal is to get away, safe and unhurt. Use any advantage you have. Fight dirty.

SCHOOL SECURITY CAMERAS GO CUTTING EDGE

By Thomas Frank

The Nashville [Tennessee] school system plans to become the first in the nation to use security cameras that spot intruders with controversial face-recognition technology.

Starting Dec. 1, the 75,000-student district will equip three schools and an administration building with cameras that can detect an unfamiliar face or someone barred from school grounds, said Ralph Thompson, assistant superintendent for student services.

"This will give us an edge in providing safety for our students and teachers," Thompson said of the $30,000 camera system. Several intruders have entered Nashville schools in the past year, he said.

A successful test in Nashville could prod other schools to try the technology, said Peter Pochowski, executive director of the National Association of School Safety and Law Enforcement Officers.

Nashville will take digital photos of students and workers at the three test schools and store them in the new camera system, Thompson said. When a camera spots a face in a school that it cannot match to a stored photo, it will alert security. The system also could detect suspended and expelled students and fired employees, Thompson said.

The technology is denounced by civil libertarians and has been discarded by police in Tampa [FL] and Virginia Beach [VA], which found face-recognition cameras in downtown districts did not help in spotting wanted criminals.

"Schools should not feel like some sort of prison," said Melissa Ngo of the Electronic Privacy Information Center.

Jay Stanley of the American Civil Liberties Union said that because the cameras identify people, their widespread use could let authorities "track you throughout the day."

Many urban schools have networks of security cameras that are monitored from a control room. Some use radio-frequency ID cards to track students as they board school buses and enter buildings. Others check visitors' names against databases of sex offenders.

—November 2, 2007

If your attacker is behind you with an arm around your neck or shoulders, use your head—literally. Smash the back of your head into the attacker's face. Your skull is a lot harder than his or her nose. Or open your mouth wide and take a big old bite of the attacker's arm. If your hands are free, grab a finger (the pinkie works best) and wrench it back.

A knee to the groin will likely disable your attacker—at least long enough for you to get away.

Whatever you have to do to break the grip, do it.

If you're facing your attacker, go for the vulnerable points. Your first instinct may be to punch your attacker in the face. That's probably not the best idea. Attacks to the face are easily blocked, and the body has far more vulnerable points to target. A solid kick, knee, fist, or elbow to the groin is likely to double over your attacker—regardless of whether it's a man or a woman. The knees and lower legs are other weak points. A solid kick to the knee is going to bring almost any attacker to the ground.

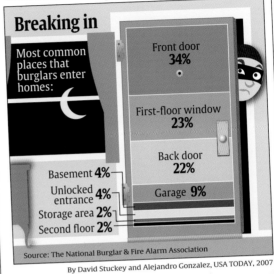

USA TODAY Snapshots®

Breaking in

Most common places that burglars enter homes:

Front door **34%**

First-floor window **23%**

Back door **22%**

Garage **9%**

Basement **4%**

Unlocked entrance **4%**

Storage area **2%**

Second floor **2%**

Source: The National Burglar & Fire Alarm Association

By David Stuckey and Alejandro Gonzalez, USA TODAY, 2007

Most break-ins are crimes of opportunity. Be sure to lock doors and secure windows to be safe.

CHECKING OUT

You've probably seen countless movies where the leading man fights off an attacker—or several attackers. He punches, jumps, and kicks his way around the room until all the bad guys are on the ground. Then he spouts off some funny one-liner and walks away, without a scratch.

THE RIGHT TO SELF-DEFENSE

What are your rights when it comes to self-defense? Are you allowed to attack or even kill anyone who threatens you? This is a question without a simple answer. Laws vary from state to state. However, most state self-defense laws contain some form of the following principle: a person who faces immediate danger from another person may use the minimum necessary force to secure his or her own safety.

What is the minimum necessary force? It's just enough force to prevent injury to yourself or someone you wish to protect, but no more. For example, if a guy comes at you with a baseball bat, you could argue that firing a gun at him is a reasonable level of force. However, if you shoot him and knock him to the ground, firing additional shots at him would be unnecessary. You could face charges for the additional shooting.

Things change a bit when it comes to intruders in your home. Many states have castle laws. Castle laws say that a person has the right to use violence to defend his or her home, or "castle." Castle laws generally ignore the rule of minimum necessary force. They allow citizens to use violent force against intruders in their own homes without the threat of heavy criminal penalties.

Build your confidence and skills by taking a self-defense class. Hopefully, you'll never have to use the techniques you learn.

That's great for a movie, but we're talking about real life. If you have to fight off an attacker, your goal isn't to be an action hero. Your goal is to get yourself safe and no more. If you knock your attacker to the ground, there's no reason for you to continue fighting. The goal is to get back to safety, not to teach your attacker a lesson. If your attacker is down, that means you should be running as fast as you can. Fighting off an attacker isn't about winning or losing. There are no style points. There are only survivors, and that's what you want to be. Get your rear end out of there and find help.

4 TIME TO *Talk*

Are you feeling threatened or worried about your safety? Talk to a trusted adult, such as a teacher or a school counselor.

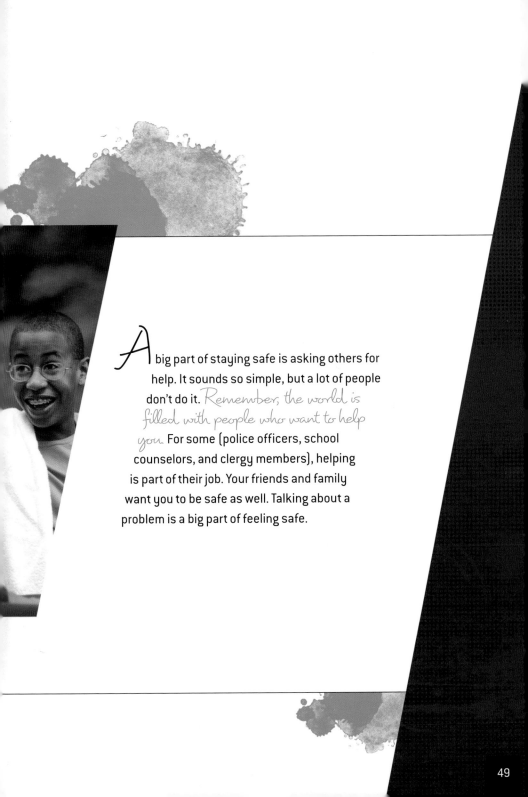

A big part of staying safe is asking others for help. It sounds so simple, but a lot of people don't do it. *Remember, the world is filled with people who want to help you.* For some (police officers, school counselors, and clergy members), helping is part of their job. Your friends and family want you to be safe as well. Talking about a problem is a big part of feeling safe.

FEELING THREATENED?

What do you do if you're feeling threatened by someone? Maybe a neighbor or family member is making inappropriate comments or touching you in an unwelcome way. Maybe a bully is stalking you through the halls of your school, and you think soon you'll get attacked. If you feel as if someone is going to hurt you, ask for help. Start with your parents. It can be hard to talk to parents about problems—especially if a threat is of a sexual nature. You may feel embarrassed or ashamed about the problem. But it's important to get past those feelings and remember that your parents want what's best for you. They have been around a lot longer than you have—use

Parents want to protect their kids. Don't be afraid to confide in a parent if you're feeling threatened.

their experience and wisdom to your advantage. If you can't talk to a parent, seek out another trusted adult. An aunt or an uncle, a favorite teacher, a school counselor or psychologist, or a clergy member are all good options.

When you talk about your problem, be specific. Say exactly why you feel threatened and by whom

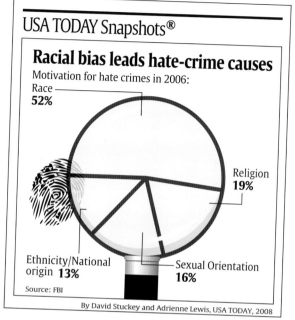

Racial bias leads hate-crime causes

Motivation for hate crimes in 2006:

Race — **52%**

Religion **19%**

Ethnicity/National origin **13%**

Sexual Orientation **16%**

Source: FBI

By David Stuckey and Adrienne Lewis, USA TODAY, 2008

Some attackers are motivated by simple hatred for a minority group. When an attack is based on bias against a person's race, religion, sexual identity, or ethnic background, it's called a hate crime. Talk to an adult immediately if you are the victim of such an attack.

you feel threatened. Don't dance around the problem. Don't speak vaguely and assume that the other person will know what you really mean. You're dealing with a serious issue, so tackle it head-on. Be clear and complete. Parents or other adults will best be able to help you if they've got all the facts—even embarrassing facts.

In some cases, talking to a trusted adult might not be enough. If someone is truly threatening your physical safety, report the problem to the authorities. If the threat is immediate, call 911. You can also call your local police department. Once again, explain the threat clearly and completely. Talking to a law enforcement officer can be intimidating. But don't let the uniform and the badge freak you out. Police officers are there to help. Keeping you safe is their job.

ONLINE HELP
FOR VICTIMS OF ABUSE

By Janet Kornblum

The nation's largest anti-sexual-assault organization will announce today that it is pioneering an Internet-based hotline to counsel abused young people, part of a new trend to reach a generation often more comfortable with texting than talking. The Rape, Abuse & Incest National Network has run a telephone hotline for 14 years. But now it hopes to reach a new generation with an anonymous instant-messaging-based hotline, says Scott Berkowitz, RAINN president.

Hotlines often serve as the first stop, whether people are reporting recent abuse or revealing old traumas for the first time. That's why anonymity is paramount [key], Berkowitz says. Trained hotline operators don't press callers to reveal personal information, but they will help connect them with authorities and counselors when appropriate, Berkowitz says.

RAINN (RAINN.org) is part of a growing number of organizations reaching out to young people reared on video games, cellphones and the Internet by testing new breeds of services. "You've got to reach out to teens where they're communicating," says Nancy Willard, author of *Cyber-Safe Kids, Cyber-Savvy Teens*.

Other recent examples include:

- The National Suicide Prevention Lifeline launched a page on MySpace last year and recently built one on rival Facebook. The social network pages lead to the telephone hotline, where people can speak with trained phone operators. It now receives 20,000 visitors a month to its website directly from MySpace. "One might say that if the Internet were a phone line, our site would be ringing off the hook," says John Draper, Lifeline manager.
- Oakland-based Internet Sexuality Information Services offers teens information about sexually transmitted diseases via cellphone text-messaging.

RAINN.org is an anti-sexual-assault organization that offers an Internet-based hotline for teens.

- The Austin-based National Domestic Violence Hotline simultaneously launched phone and Internet hotlines for teen dating violence last year, says CEO Sheryl Cates. "The majority (of teens) want to communicate online," she says.

Typing on a computer screen to an unseen and unheard voice can make it easier to discuss painful subjects, Willard says. Adding a new way to discuss sexual abuse is "a stroke of genius," says Kathryn Seifert, a psychologist and author in Salisbury, MD.

Stacy Bogart, 25, who called the RAINN hotline for emotional support after she reported being raped in 2002, says she would have loved to turn to an Internet hotline.

"This is groundbreaking," she says. "It is going to help so many people. Rape is such a personal thing. If the survivor feels more comfortable IMing because they feel it's less personal, then great."

—April 14, 2008

Always report an attack to the police. Tell the officer every detail about the attacker that you can remember.

REPORTING AN ATTACK

If you do get attacked, report it. Suppose you were walking home from a movie one night and a man came up behind you and mugged you. The attack left you with a black eye, and the criminal took your wallet and your cell phone.

You need to report the crime immediately. Find another phone and dial 911. The dispatcher will probably send an officer out to you. His or her job is to gather information about the crime. This is where you can make a big difference—especially if you remained aware during the attack.

The officer will ask for a description of the attacker. The more detail you can provide, the better. Tell the officer everything you can remember. Was the attacker tall or short? Fat or thin? Note hair color and hairstyle as well as skin color. Did the attacker have any distinguishing marks or features? Maybe you noticed a mole, a tattoo, or a scar. How was the attacker dressed? Was a car or another vehicle involved? What color was it? Did it have two doors or four doors? Were you able to read the license plate number? Any detail can help. If you stay aware during an attack and note details about the attacker, the police will have a much better chance of making an arrest.

Officers will also want to collect any evidence of an attack, so don't disturb the crime scene before they arrive. If an attacker broke your window, don't clean up the glass. Don't take a shower or wash yourself off, because the attacker might have left evidence on your body. This evidence might include some of the attacker's hair, skin, blood, saliva, or other bodily fluids. These substances contain genetic material called DNA, which police might be able to use to identify your attacker.

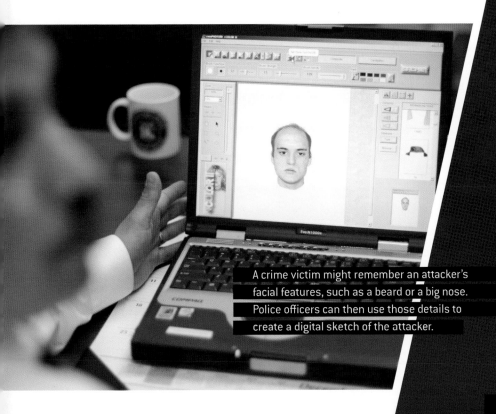

A crime victim might remember an attacker's facial features, such as a beard or a big nose. Police officers can then use those details to create a digital sketch of the attacker.

CALLING FOR HELP

If you've been the victim of a crime—or fear that you might be—check out the list of organizations below. They operate hotlines staffed by trained professionals.

Hate Crime Hotline 1-800-616-4283
This hotline provides support for victims of hate crimes, focusing on crimes against gays and lesbians.

National Center for Missing and Exploited Children
1-800-843-5678
This hotline is for reporting children that have been taken from their homes, either by strangers or by family members (such as a parent unlawfully taking children from the other parent after a divorce). Call this number if you suspect a child has been taken from his or her home unlawfully or is suffering from any sort of abuse.

National Child Abuse Hotline 1-800-422-4453
This hotline is dedicated to the prevention of child abuse. If you or someone you know is being abused, operators may be able to help.

National Domestic Violence Hotline 1-800-799-7233
Victims of domestic abuse can find help at this hotline.

National Suicide Prevention Lifeline 1-800-273-8255
Many victims of violent attacks feel depressed or suicidal. If you find yourself thinking about suicide, call this number for help.

Many organizations run telephone hotlines for crime victims.

THE HEALING PROCESS

Recovering from an attack can be a long, hard process. Many victims feel violated and have trouble trusting others. They may not feel safe among strangers. Victims of sexual assault may find themselves uncomfortable around people who remind them of the attacker. *An attack of any sort can leave deep emotional scars.*

The first step in healing is talking about what happened and about your feelings. Maybe you just need to open up to a good friend or a family member. Another option is a victim's hotline or website. The staff members there will help you talk through your ordeal. Some victims may need professional help to address feelings of fear, violation, and mistrust. Trained therapists or psychologists know how to guide victims through the healing process. Seeing a therapist or a psychologist might feel a little scary, but it can be the key to feeling like your old self again.

EPILOGUE
CHOOSING *Safety*

The world will always be a risky place. But you can minimize the risk by using safety smarts.

The world can be a scary place sometimes. Most people are good at heart and mean you no harm. But all it takes is one bad seed to put your safety or even your life at risk. There's no way to take all the risk out of your life. *Part of being alive is taking risks.* But there's a big difference between smart risks and dumb risks.

The choices you make go a long way to keeping you safe. Trying out for the school lacrosse team might be a good risk, even though you could be hurt while playing. Speeding down a busy highway while composing a text message on your phone is a bad risk. You're just asking for trouble.

Think of all the safety choices you make over the course of a day. Something as simple as looking both ways before you cross a street is a safety choice. Choosing to go to a movie with friends instead of heading out alone for a long walk after dark is another. You might choose to walk away from a bully rather than pick a fight or to log off an online chat room as soon as a stranger starts to make you feel uncomfortable.

Of course, all the good choices in the world can't keep you safe all the time. **Be aware of your surroundings and trust your instincts.** Project a strong and confident image. If you *look* like a victim, you're more likely to become one. When facing a threat, use your voice. Shout and scream for help if the situation looks desperate. Get away from danger as quickly as you can and fight only as a last resort.

If someone has hurt you, don't be afraid to talk about it. Talking is a big part of the healing process and can help you feel safe again. *Remember, there's a world full of people who want to help you.* As scary as life can be sometimes, that is a comforting thought.

GLOSSARY

BULLYING: abusive, threatening, or violent treatment

DISTRACTED DRIVING: operating a motor vehicle while not giving one's full attention to the road. Texting and talking on a cell phone while driving are forms of distracted driving.

DNA: genetic material contained in the cells of humans and other living things. Each person's DNA is unique, so if police officers can match DNA from a crime scene to DNA from a suspect, they can positively identify a criminal.

FIGHT OR FLIGHT: a survival response that kicks in when a person is in danger. Chemicals surge into the bloodstream, preparing the person to either fight for survival or run to safety.

HATE CRIME: an attack on a person based on a bias against his or her race, ethnicity, sexual orientation, religion, or other social characteristic

INSTINCT: a thought or a feeling based on intuition rather than on hard logic

PSYCHOLOGIST: a professional trained in the science of the mind and behavior. A psychologist can help victims of assault or abuse heal emotionally.

SEXUAL PREDATOR: a person who seeks to instigate sexual contact with others in a predatory manner, often targeting minors or vulnerable adults

SUICIDE: the act of deliberately taking one's own life

SELECTED BIBLIOGRAPHY

Dyer, Gerri M., ed. *Safe, Smart and Self-Reliant: Personal Safety for Women and Children*. Rockville, MD: Safety Press, 1996.

Lines, Dennis. *The Bullies: Understanding Bullies and Bullying*. Philadelphia: Jessica Kingsley Publishers, 2008.

Maier, Bill, ed. *Help! My Child Is Being Bullied*. Carol Stream, IL: Tyndale House Publishers, 2006.

McCallum, Paul. *The Parent's Guide to Teaching Self-Defense*. Cincinnati: Betterway Books, 1994.

Nemours Foundation. "KidsHealth." *Nemours Foundation*. 2011. http://www .kidshealth.org (August 9, 2011).

Sanders, Pete, and Steve Myers. *Personal Safety*. Brookfield, CT: Copper Beech Books, 1999.

Stoneburner, Lee. *Personal Safety Tips for Everyday Living*. Lincoln, NE: Writer's Showcase, 2002.

FURTHER INFORMATION

Anderson, Judith. *Know the Facts about Personal Safety.* New York: Rosen
    Central, 2010. Short chapters give readers tips for a wide range of safety
    practices, from safety on the Internet to safety in the water.

Colt, James P. *Cyberpredators.* New York: Chelsea House, 2011. The Internet can
    be a dangerous place for kids and teens. Read more about cyberpredators,
    the threats they bring, and how to deal with them.

Doeden, Matt. *Conflict Resolution Smarts: How to Communicate, Negotiate,
    Compromise, and More.* Minneapolis: Twenty-First Century Books, 2012.
    This book gives helpful tips on avoiding conflicts, managing them when
    they do occur, and ensuring that all parties feel good about the outcome.

It's My Life
    http://pbskids.org/itsmylife
    This website is packed with information for teens on everything from
    dealing with bullies to handling emotions such as anger and depression.

Love Is Respect
    http://blog.loveisrespect.org
    Read about safety issues, learn the basics of safe dating, and find out if
    you're in an abusive dating relationship.

Marzilli, Alan. *The Internet and Crime.* New York: Chelsea House, 2010.
    This debate book discusses a wide range of Internet threats and how they
    should be dealt with, both at an individual and criminal level.

National Center for Victims of Crime
    http://www.ncvc.org/ncvc/Main.aspx
    This site is a great resource for people who have been the victim of a crime.
    Learn about your rights as a victim, healing strategies, and much more.

Nelson, Sara. *Stay Safe: How You Can Keep Out of Harm's Way.* Minneapolis:
    Lerner Publications Company, 2009.
    Through easy-to-read text, photos, and illustrations, Nelson covers a wide
    range of safety threats and offers a five-step system for dealing with them.

NetSmartz
http://www.netsmartz.org/Teens
NetSmartz offers online safety tips and stories from real teens who have
dealt with threats. It even has a tip line where you can report cyberbullying.

Rooney, Anne. *Bullying*. Mankato, MN: Arcturus, 2010.
Rooney discusses the growing problem of bullying, why it happens, and
strategies kids can use to deal with it.

SafeTeens
http://www.safeteens.com
Read articles on a wide range of teen safety issues. Read tips on staying
safe and learn more about resources available to help keep teens safe.

Self Defense for Teens
http://assaultprevention.info/?p=3878
How can you protect yourself from an attack? Check out this site for
detailed information on how to defend yourself and others.

Stop Bullying
http://www.stopbullying.gov
This site provides information from various U.S. government agencies on
the problem of bullying and tells how kids and adults can prevent it.

TeensHealth—Staying Safe
http://kidshealth.org/teen/safety
Check out this site for tips on safety in situations such as driving or playing
sports, and learn some basic first-aid tips.

Winkler, Kathleen. *Bullying: How to Deal with Taunting, Teasing, and Tormenting*.
Berkeley Heights, NJ: Enslow Publishers, 2005.
This book is packed with information on bullying and the kids who do it. It
also offers coping strategies for victims.

LERNER

SOURCE™

Expand learning beyond the printed book. Download free, complementary
educational resources for this book from our website, www.lerneresource.com.

INDEX

ABOUT THE AUTHOR

Matt Doeden has written and edited hundreds of nonfiction books. Lots of them are on high-interest topics such as cars, sports, and airplanes. He also writes and edits books about geography, science, and math. He lives with his family in Minnesota.